ANIMALS

Ros Pilcher

Everyone should speak a foreign language

Primary Language Publications Activity Books

Primary Language Publications have produced a series of language activity books for children aged 7-11 years. Written by primary language teachers to support early language acquisition at home, the series follows the QCA scheme of work for language learning at Key Stage 2.

The books combine simple text and amusing pictures to enable the child to learn from word and picture association. The stickers, certificate, child friendly characters and illustrations make learning a language at home both easy and fun.

There are 10 activity books, all available in French, German, Spanish, Italian and Gujarati, which:

- help the child to learn the core KS2 language vocabulary
- give opportunities for repeated, enjoyable practice
- give the child confidence and satisfaction in their new found skill.

A self teach approach, with complimentary support available on-line from qualified language teachers (www.clubs4children.org), allows even those parents who did not study the language at school to support their child at home. Together with notes and guidance for parents, this will ensure that you give your child the best possible start in learning a foreign language. Further resources can be purchased on-line again at www.clubs4children.org.

Good luck   Bonne Chance
Viel Glück   Buena Suerte   Buona Fortuna

ISBN 0-9547980-4-X
Copyright © by C. & R. Pilcher

All rights reserved. No part of this publication may be reproduced, stored in a retrieval system, or transmitted, in any form or by any means, without prior written permission of the publisher, nor be otherwise circulated in any form of binding or cover other than that in which it is published and without a similar condition being imposed on the subsequent purchaser.

Published in Great Britain 2005

Published by Primary Language Publications, Highfields, Rempstone Road, Belton, Leicestershire, England LE12 9XA. Telephone: 01509 502314.

Printed by The Shepshed Knight Printing Service Limited. Telephone: 01509 502246

JE ME PRÉSENTE ET MES AMIS...

Je muh pray-zont ay mez am-mee...
Let me introduce myself and my friends...

Salut! Je m'appelle
Laurent

Salut! Je m'appelle
Patrice

Salut! Je m'appelle
Francoise

Bonjour! Je m'appelle
Sophie

3
Trois

ET AUSSI...
ay o-see
and also...

Bonjour! Je m'appelle Anne-Marie

Bonjour! Je m'appelle Pierre

Now you are our friends, perhaps you would like to draw a picture of yourself and write your name below

----

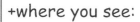

Now to complete this workbook

+where you see:
- a box with the French word below draw the correct picture
- a picture, write the French word on the dotted line underneath

+ you will find new French words at the bottom of the page with their meaning in English and how to say them in phonetics
+ if you forget a French word just look back through the book
+ there is a full vocabulary list at the back of the book

Je m'appelle	juh ma-pel	My name is ...
Bonjour	bon-jor	Hello
Salut	sal-oo	Hi there

4
Quatre

QUI EST-CE?
key ess
Who is it?

Elle s'appelle

Bonjour ---------------

Salut ------------------

Il s'appelle

Bonne chance	bon shons	Good luck
Amusez-vous bien	am-moo-zay voo be-an	Have fun
Elle s'appelle	ell sap-pel	Her name is....
Il s'appelle	eel sap-pel	His name is....

5
Cinq

JE VAIS AU ZOO ET JE VOIS

juh vay o zoo ay juh vwa
I go to the zoo and I see

un lion   un serpent   _____

_____   _____   un ours

Un éléphant	un ellay-fon	elephant
Un lion	un lee-on	lion
Un tigre	un tee-gra	tiger
Un serpent	un sair-pon	snake
Un ours	un oors	bear
Une girafe	oon jee-raff	giraffe

6
Six

ET AUSSI
ay o-see And also

un chameau

un kangourou

----

un rhinocéros

Un panda	un pon-da	panda
Un kangourou	un kong-a-roo	kangaroo
Un rhinocéros	un rin-o-sir-os	rhinoceros
Un chameau	un sha-mow	camel
Un pingouin	un pin-gwan	penguin
Un hippopotame	un ee-po-pot-am	hippopotamus

MES ANIMAUX FAVORITS AU ZOO

mays anee-mo fav-or-ree o zoo

My favourite zoo animals

La liste
d'Anne-Marie
un tigre
un chameau
un pingouin

La liste de
Patrice
un lion
un ours
un serpent

La liste de
Françoise
un éléphant
un kangourou
une girafe

Draw our French friends' favourite zoo animals
underneath the lists which they have written for you.

LE DÎNER DES ANIMAUX

luh dee-nay days anee-mo
Dinner time for the animals

Le Dîner des animaux

le chameau	14.00 heures
l' éléphant	12.00 heures
la girafe	10.00 heures
le lion	16.00 heures
l'ours	13.00 heures
le serpent	15.00 heures
le tigre	11.00 heures

10.00 heures

11.00 heures

12.00 heures

13.00 heures

14.00 heures

15.00 heures

16.00 heures

Pierre wants to see all the animals being fed. Complete his diary above, writing in French the name of the animal being fed at that time.

9
Neuf

LES MOTS CROISÉS

10
Dix

LES ANIMAUX DE PATRICE

lays anee-mo duh pat-reece

Patrice's animals

Il s'appelle Pierre   un rat   Il _____ Charles   _____ Minou

Il _____ Paul   Elle _____ Suzanne   un chien / Il _____ Charles

Un poisson	un pwass-on	fish
Un perroquet	un perrokay	parrot
Un rat	un ra	rat
Une souris	oon soo-ree	mouse
Un chien	un she-an	dog
Un chat	un sha	cat

11
Onze

ET VOICI MES ANIMAUX

ay vwa-see mays anee-mo

And here are my animals

C'est moi

_____ _____
_____ s'appelle _____ s'appelle
_____ _____

Draw a picture of you and your animals and write their names below

ET JE VOUDRAIS   ay juh voo-dray   and I would like

_____   _____   _____

_____   _____   _____

12
Douze

C'est moi   say mwa   that's me

J'AI
jay I have

"J'ai .... "

" .... une souris"

"J'ai .... "

" .... un chat"

"J'ai un serpent"

" .... un poisson"

"J'ai .... "

C'est moi

Mon animal
My pet

13
Treize

IL A

eel a **He has**

........................un chien

Il a................................

........................un chat

Il a................................

Il a................................

Draw a boy in each of the boxes on the left of the page and his pet in each of the boxes on the right. Complete the sentences.

14
Quatorze

ELLE A
ell a She has

Elle a ....

.... un serpent

.... un perroquet

Elle a ....

Elle a ....

Draw a girl in each of the boxes on the left of the page and his pet in each of the boxes on the right. Complete the sentences.

15
Quinze

IL VA À LA FERME ET IL VOIT

Eel va a la fairm ay eel vwa
He goes to the farm and he sees

_____

un cheval

un agneau

_____

un mouton

_____

Un agneau	un an-yo	lamb
Un mouton	un moo-ton	sheep
Un cheval	un shev-al	horse
Un poulet	un poo-lay	hen
Une vache	oon vash	cow
Une chèvre	oon shev-ra	goat

ET AUSSI
ay o-see And also

une oie

une dinde

Un cochon	un cosh-on	pig
Un taureau	un tor-row	bull
Un coq	un cock	cockerel
Une dinde	oon dand	turkey
Une oie	oon wa	goose
Un âne	un an	donkey

17
Dix-sept

ELLE VA AU PARC ET ELLE VOIT

el va o parc ay ell vwa
She goes to the park and she sees

un hérisson

une coccinelle

_____

un oiseau

_____

une chenille

Un oiseau	un waz-o	bird
Un canard	un ca-nar	duck
Un lapin	un lap-pan	rabbit
Une chenille	oon shuh-neel	caterpillar
Une coccinelle	oon cock-sea-nell	ladybird
Un hérisson	un ay-ree-son	hedgehog

18
Dix-huit

ET AUSSI
ay o-see And also

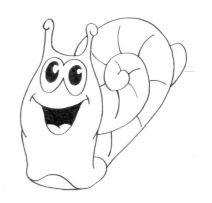

_____   un caneton   _____

une guêpe   _____   les têtards

Un caneton	un canuh-ton	duckling
Un cygne	un seen-ya	swan
Un escargot	un es-kar-go	snail
Une guêpe	oon gep	wasp
Une grenouille	oon grun-wee	frog
Les têtards	lay tet-ar	tadpoles

19
Dix-neuf

AU SECOURS!
o suh-cor Help!

The animals have escaped. Help to round them up by writing their names in French in the pens next to their correct home.

JE SUIS

je swee I am

"miaou
Je suis
........................"

"grrrrr....
....
un lion"

"bêêêêêêê
Je suis
........................"

"sssssss......
Je suis
........................"

"meuh
....
........................"

"ouah, ouah
....
........................"

"coin, coin
....
........................"

"cui, cui
....
........................"

21
Vingt-et-un

LES ANIMAUX PARLENT

lays anee-mo parl

The animals speak

miaou
mee-ow

ouah, ouah
wa-wa

cot, cot, codète
cot-cot-cod-ett

cui, cui
cwee, cwee

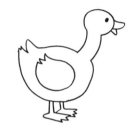

coin, coin
cwan cwan

croac croac
crow-ack crow-Oack

meuh
moo

hiiiiii
heeeee

nique nique
neek neek

bêêêêêêê
bair

Anne-Marie is confused about which animal makes which sound.
Sort her out!

22
Vingt-deux

QUÉST-CE QUE C'EST?
keska say What is it?

C'est un éléphant?
Non, c'est un rhinocéros.

C'est un serpent?
Oui, c'est un serpent.

C'est un lion?
....

C'est un souris?
Non, c'est un rat.

C'est une giraffe?
Non, c'est un tigre.

C'est un coq?
Non, c'est un canard.

| Oui | we | yes |
| Non | non | no |

Patrice is confused about which animals are which.
Sort him out!

Vingt-trois

TROUVE LES MOTS

R	P	I	N	G	U	I	N	I	P	A	N	D	A
C	L	L	E	P	O	I	C	O	C	H	O	N	U
H	O	I	E	O	I	T	R	P	E	N	O	G	O
A	M	O	N	I	S	O	T	C	O	Q	F	U	I
T	M	N	T	S	O	U	R	I	S	U	B	C	S
G	T	U	J	S	C	R	T	N	A	W	E	Y	E
I	U	W	E	O	Y	S	Y	G	O	I	N	E	A
D	K	U	T	N	D	E	C	H	I	E	N	I	U
I	P	G	I	R	A	F	E	S	T	R	E	G	B
N	O	U	G	U	O	R	P	C	H	E	V	A	L
D	U	O	R	P	E	N	T	I	O	R	U	E	P
E	L	T	E	I	Y	G	U	L	A	P	I	N	O
S	E	E	G	H	F	A	E	R	Y	W	F	B	N
M	T	Y	U	Y	V	A	C	H	E	O	M	I	S

LION POULET
TIGRE VACHE
OURS COQ
GIRAFE OIE
PANDA DINDE
PINGUIN CHIEN
COCHON POISSON
CHEVAL OISEAU
SOURIS CHAT
LAPIN

24
Vingt-quatre

OH LA LA!
O la la Oh dear!

The animals have escaped again!
Is Patrice playing a practical joke?
Join up the animals to their correct homes.

25
Vingt-cinq

LES MOTS CROISÉS

Across

1    8

4    10

7    11

Down

1    5

2    6

3    9

26
Vingt-six

PATRICE AIME LES INSECTES

Pat-reese em lays an-sect
Patrice likes insects

_____

Une mouche

_____

Une sauterelle

Un phasme — _____

Un phasme

Un ver	un vair	worm
Une mouche	oon moosh	fly
Une araignée	oon a-ren-yay	spider
Une cigale	oon see-gall	cricket
Une sauterelle	oon sow-ter-rel	grasshopper
Un phasme	un fas-muh	stick insect

27
Vingt-sept

SOPHIE AIME LES OISEAUX

Sophie em lays waz-o
Sophie likes birds

Une merle

_____

Une colombe

_____

Un rouge-gorge

_____

Une pie	oon pee	magpie
Une merle	oon mearl	blackbird
Un pigeon	un pee-jhon	wood pigeon
Une colombe	oon col-lomb	dove
Un rouge-gorge	un rooj-gorj	robin
Un corbeau	un cor-bow	crow

Answer Section including Parents' Notes

It is important that children enjoy Early Language Learning and this activity book enables your child to learn to speak, listen, read and write in the target language, all key areas at G.C.S.E. Travel broadens the mind and this generation of young travellers will have opportunities to travel that few of us may have had.

This section has been written for parents, but with the child in mind and provides answers and guidelines for parents, including grammar points and in some instances an extension exercise. It is therefore important to read the parents' notes for that page before allowing your child to complete the page. The self teach nature of the activity book does mean that, depending on the age and ability of your child, he may well manage to complete the pages alone and therefore parental input may be minimalized.

Always correct your child's work and praise his efforts. This will encourage your child to enjoy Early Language Learning. Draw your child's attention to the vocabulary section at the end of the book and at the bottom of certain pages and if there are mistakes, point these out to your child in order that he does not make the mistake again.

We hope that this section is useful and we wish you and your child all the best of luck.

Page 3
This page introduces the characters which you will meet in the book as well as teaching your child how to introduce himself.
Encourage your child to use these examples to learn how to say his name, then take on the role of other people to reinforce the expression:
Je m'appelle   juh m'appel   My name is ....
Draw your child's attention to the vocabulary list at the back of the book and, depending on the age and ability of the child, perhaps suggest you 'tick off' each word as you meet it. What an achievement when you have 'ticked off' every word.

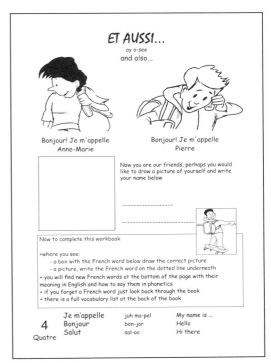

Page 4
It is very important to read the information box with your child as it informs you how to complete each page.
The activity on this page provides practice writing in the target language. Ensure that your child takes his time and encourage him to check his spelling using the vocabulary at the bottom of the page.

Your child is referred to in these notes as 'he' purely for the sake of simplicity and brevity, with no offence intended to the girls!

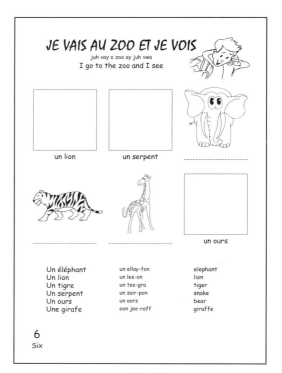

Page 5
This activity introduces the third person, 'Il' and 'Elle', 'He' and 'She'. Ask your child to find the name of each character, then introduce him or her as the third person. Encourage your child to use the vocabulary at the bottom of the page to say 'he/she is called' in French. Your child will then be able to write the characters' names in the space provided. Ask your child to repeat what he has written as this will reinforce this grammar point.
Award one of the brightly coloured stickers.

Page 6
This page introduces your child to animals at the zoo. Encourage your child to use the phonetics to pronounce the new vocabulary at the bottom of the page before attempting to complete the exercise. Repetition helps to reinforce vocabulary Highlight the article 'un' and 'une' that comes before the noun and explain that in French nouns are either masculine of feminine. Masculine nouns take 'un' whilst feminine nouns take 'une'. It is very important to learn the article with the noun.

Page 7
Always encourage your child to read the title, phonetics and translation on every page. Look closely at the title on page 6 and then on page 7. On page 6 Anne-Marie must use the pronoun Je which translates as I whereas on page 7 she is talking about Sophie and therefore must use the pronoun Elle which translates as She.
Once again, encourage your child to repeat the vocabulary, using the phonetics and again highlight the article. If your child feels sufficiently confident, cover the English word and ask what the French word means in English. Most animal words in French are similar to the English word.

Page 8
Revise the vocabulary taught on the previous pages and use the phonetics to ensure that the word is correctly pronounced
This activity revises the vocabulary learnt to date. Encourage your child to attempt to complete the page without looking back at the vocabulary on the previous pages but if your child needs to, allow him to do so. Ask him to list separately his favourite zoo animals. You can use our on-line dictionary to find any animal vocabulary you require www.clubs4children.org.

30 Trente

Page 9
On this page your child is introduced to the 24 hour clock and how to write the time in French. In French, rather that writing 11.00 am, the French write 11h00, 'h' stands for 'heures', which means 'hours' in English.

Page 10
Before completing the crossword, read through the vocabulary again on pages 6, 7 and 8. Then cover the vocabulary at the bottom of each page and for each animal ask the question:
Qu'est ce que c'est   Keska say   What is it?
He must reply: C'est un lion   set un lion   It is a lion
Point to each animal in turn and ask the same question as previously.
Award a sticker for successful completion of this section to chart your progress.

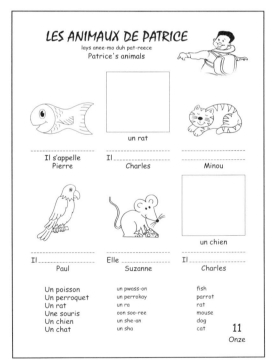

Page 11
Again, encourage your child to read the title on each page. Now we are talking about Patrice's animals. Highlight the article before the noun and point out that Patrice has more than one animal and therefore he must use 'les'. Encourage him to repeat this new vocabulary and always use the phonetics to ensure correct pronunciation.
You may like to make a card game. You will need two squares of paper or card on which you will need to draw a picture of each animal. If you write the word in French on the reverse, these can be used as flash cards. Play as Snap and shout out: C'est moi!   say mwa   That's me!

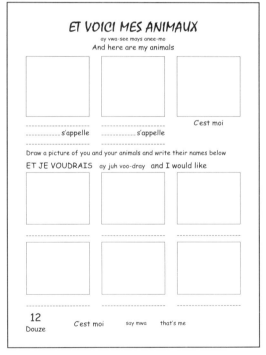

Page 12
On this page, your child talks about his own animals. We meet the possessive adjective 'mes' which goes with a plural noun and which means 'my'.
Ask your child to draw a picture of himself and two pets, imagined if necessary, and to write what each one is on the dotted lines below. You can use our on-line dictionary to find any animal vocabulary you require www.clubs4children.org. We have already met il/elle s'appelle on page 5 and do refer him back to this earlier page if necessary. Notes continued on following page.
Award a sticker for this section to chart your progress.

31 Trent-et-un

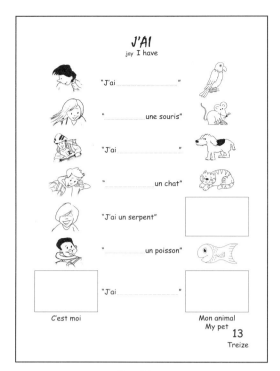

Page 13
Highlight 'je voudrais' in the second section. Explain that this means 'I would like' and say that this is a useful phrase to learn, as it can be applied in many other circumstances. Your child may have already used this phrase in our Activity Book 4- Shopping.
The following three pages introduce the verb Avoir – to have. Read aloud the title, phonetics and translation. Here we learn how to say 'I have'. This is the first person of Avoir- to have. Notes continued on following page.

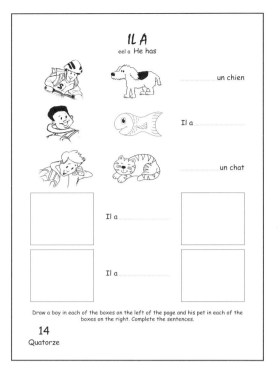

Page 14
Complete the sentences on this page, the previous page and the following page and then with the help of the phonetics read these sentences aloud.
On this page and the following page, your child is introduced to the third person of Avoir which translates as either 'he has' or 'she has'. We already know that 'Il' and 'elle' translate as 'he' and 'she'. Avoir is an important verb – to make the past tense we must use this verb – and it is therefore essential that your child takes time completing these pages.
Always encourage your child to check spellings and always praise his efforts.

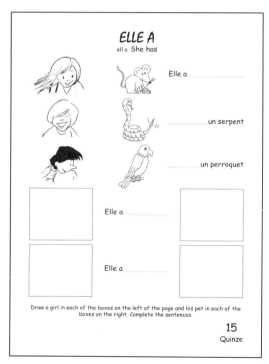

Page 15
Suggest that you 'test' how well he remembers the vocabulary he has met to date. Draw his attention to the vocabulary list at the back of the book and suggest that you tick off each word each time he answers correctly and continue to do this at every opportunity. It would be a shame not to do so. Your child – and you too- have every right to feel pleased with your efforts.
Children love to record their attempts at speaking a foreign language - if you have the technology to do so, record your child's pronunciation of the vocabulary taught to date.
Award a sticker for this section to chart your progress.

Page 16
This page introduces the verbs Aller – to go and Voir – to see. Read aloud the title, phonetics and translation. Here we learn how to say 'Il va' and 'Il voit' which translates as he goes and he sees.
Repeat the vocabulary using the phonetics. Highlight the article (un/une) and the importance of learning the article with the noun.

32 Trente-deux

Page 17
This page continues with animals on the farm. Ensure that your child reads aloud this new vocabulary before completing the page.
For this game you will need again two sets of cards but without the written word on the reverse. Spread the cards out on a table face down and take it in turns to turn one over and then to find the matching pair.
If successful, you can have another go and do remember to shout out: C'est moi! say mwa That's me!
It is important that your child enjoys learning French as through enjoyment his confidence and self-esteem will grow.
Award a sticker for this section to chart your progress.

Page 18
On this page and the next page, your child meets another new vocabulary. Again encourage your child to read the title, phonetics and translation before starting the activity. This page re-introduces the verbs Aller – to go and Voir – to see. Here we learn how to say 'Elle va' and 'Elle voit' which translates as she goes and she sees.

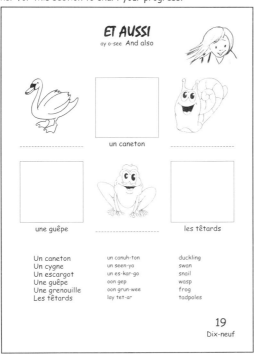

Page 19
Depending on the age and ability of your child, systematically go through each word on these pages and other pages. If this activity sustains your child's interest, check that he knows how to translate each one from French to English and English to French.
Ask your child to reply in English:
Une chenille , qu'est-ce que c'est en anglais? oon shuh-neel keska say on on-glay
What is it in English?
Now, ask him to reply in French:
A caterpillar , qu'est-ce que c'est en francais? Keska say on fron-say. What is it in French?
C'est une chenille Set tun sha It's a caterpillar
Award a sticker for this section to chart your progress.

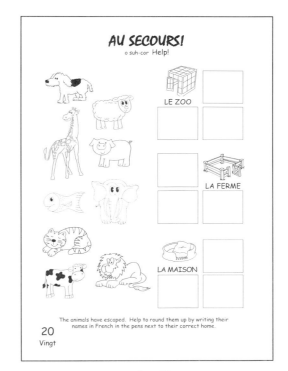

Page 20
This page is fun and doesn't rely on any French other than remembering La Ferme is the farm (your child could probably guess at this!) and La Maison is the house. A maisonette is the name given to a very small house in English and is derived from the French.
Award a sticker for this section to chart your progress.

33 Trente-trois

Page 21
This page and the next introduce the verb Etre - to be. Here we learn how to say 'Je suis' which translates as 'I am'.
This will be an important verb to learn as it is also used to make the past tense in French. For further practice of the verb Etre, go to Activity Book 3- Me and My Family.
Encourage your child to complete these pages and then with the help of the phonetics read the sentences aloud.
Always encourage your child to check spellings as there is no excuse for spelling mistakes as all the vocabulary is listed in the book.
Award a sticker for this section to chart your progress.

Page 22
Again, encourage your child to read the title, phonetics, translation and the instructions before attempting the activity. Emphasise the fact that although French animals make the same sounds as English animals, the French interpret the sounds differently and they are therefore spelt differently. Encourage your child to use the phonetics to make the sounds the animals make before completing the activity.

Page 23
You may have already asked this question before completing the activity on pages 10 and 19. Before attempting to complete this page, point to each picture and ask your child: Qu'est ce que c'est Keska say What is it? He must reply: C'est un lion set un lion It is a lion. If he is having difficulty, encourage him to refer back to this vocabulary. Then point to each animal in turn and ask: C'est un elephant? Set un ay-lay-fon Is it an elephant?
If it is, he replies: Oui, c'est un elephant we set un ellay-fon Yes, it's an elephant. If it isn't, he replies: Non, c'est un rhinoceros non set un rin-o-say-ross No, it's a rhinoceros. Then, encourage him to complete the page.

Page 24
Before your child completes the word search, point to each word and ask: Qu'est ce que c'est? keska say What is it?
Again, depending on the age and ability of your child, systematically go through each word on these and other pages. If this activity sustains your child's interest, check that he knows how to translate each one from French to English and English to French.
See notes for page 19.

34 Trente-quatre

Page 25
This page again revises the animal vocabulary and is similar to the activity on page 20. All children are familiar with the tune Three Blind Mice and will enjoy the simplicity of this rhyme in French.

Un, deux, trois	un, duh, twa	one, two, three
Un, deux, trois	un, duh, twa	one, two, three
Quatre, cinq, six	catr, sank, sees	four, five, six
Quatre, cinq, six	catr, sank, sees	four, five, six
Sept, huit, neuf souris	set, weet, nerf soo-ree	seven, eight, nine mice
Sept, huit, neuf souris	set, weet, nerf soo-ree	seven, eight, nine mice
Dix souris	dees soo-ree	ten mice
Dix souris.	dees soo-ree	ten mice

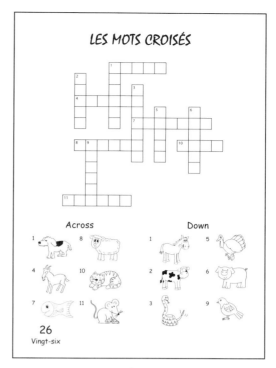

Page 26
Again more vocabulary revision. Encourage your child to go through the vocabulary with you before attempting to complete the cross-word in French. It is necessary to stress the importance of spelling words correctly. Always check your child's spelling and praise his/her efforts.
Choose some famous cartoon animals and ask:

Donald Duck, il est un lion?	eel et tun lee-on	he is a lion?
Non, il est un canard.	non eel et tun can-nar	No, he is a duck.
Mickey, il est un souris?	eel et un soor-ree	Yes, he is a mouse

Page 27
Most children are fascinated by insects- and on this page Patrice shares his insect collection with you. This page introduces the verb- Aimer to like which is practised further in Activity Book 9- School. Here we learn how to say I like or J'aime.
You may like to play this game which is a variation of Noughts and Crosses and requires the child to correctly guess the square in which the animal is hidden in order to have their nought or cross!
Draw out a nine square grid and make a card for any nine animals. Shuffle the cards in order that neither player knows where each card has been placed. The first player guesses which animal one of the turned over cards might be, saying, for example, C'est un lion. The player then turns over that card and, if correct, replaces it with either a nought or a cross. These cards can again be very easily made. The first player to get a full line of noughts or crosses wins. C'est le gagnant say luh gan-yon the winner

Page 28
Sophie likes birds - Elle aime les oiseaux. Pigeons very often race large distances - this pigeon has come first in his race. Magpies are thieves whilst crows are large and quite scary! This one certainly is! Award a final sticker and then the certificate.

Très bien!

35 Trente-cinq

VOCABULARY LIST

Put a tick in the box next to each word as you learn it.
See how quickly you can learn new words!

French	Phonetics	English	French	Phonetics	English
un agneau	un an-yo	lamb	un kangourou	un kong-a-roo	kangaroo
un âne	un an	donkey	un lapin	un lap-pan	rabbit
mon animal	mon anee-mal	my animal	un lion	un lee-on	lion
les animaux	lays anee-mo	animals	la maison	la mezon	house
Une araigné	a-ren-yay	spider	une merle	oon mearl	blackbird
un canard	un can-ar	duck	une mouche	oon moosh	fly
un caneton	un canuh-ton	duckling	un mouton	un moo-ton	sheep
un chameau	un sha-mow	camel	une oie	oon wa	goose
un chat	un sha	cat	un oiseau	un waz-o	bird
une chenille	oo shuh-neel	caterpillar	un ours	un oors	bear
un cheval	un shev-al	horse	un panda	un pon-da	panada
un chèvre	un shev-ra	goat	un perroquet	un perro-kay	parrot
une cigale	oon see-gall	cricket	un phasme	un fasm-uh	stick insect
un chien	un she-an	dog	une pie	oon pee	magpie
un cochon	un cosh-on	pig	un pigeon	un pee-jhon	pigeon
une coccinelle	oon cock-see-nell	ladybird	un pingouin	un pin-gwan	penguin
une colombe	oon col-lomb	dove	un poisson	un pwass-on	fish
un corbeau	un cor-bow	crow	un poulet	un poo-lay	chicken
un coq	un cock	cockerel	un rat	un ra	rat
un cygne	un seen-ya	swan	un rhinocéros	un rin-o-say-ross	rhinoceros
une dinde	oon dand	turkey	un rouge-gorge	oon rooj-gorj	robin
le dîner	luh dee-nay	dinner	une sauterelle	oon sow-ter-rol	grasshopper
un é éphant	un ellay-fon	elephant	un serpent	un sair-pon	snake
un escargot	un es-kar-go	snail	une souris	oon soo-ree	mouse
la ferme	la fairm	farm	un taureau	un tor-row	bull
une girafe	oon jeer-aff	giraffe	es têtards	ay tet-ar	tadpoles
une grenouille	oon grun-wee	frog	un tigre	un tee-gra	tiger
une guêpe	oon gep	wasp	un ver	un vair	worm
un hérisson	un ay-ree-son	hedgehog	une vache	oon vash	cow
un hippopotame	un ee-po-pot-am	hippopotamus	le zoo	luh zoo	zoo